The Power Tower

To Goldie:
Be Blessed!
Jackie

The Power Tower

Prayer is the Tower to Power

Jacquelyn Bryant

II KINGS 2:13, 14

END TIME WAVE PUBLICATIONS

East Orange, New Jersey

The Power Tower

Prayer is the Tower to Power

 Published by END TIME WAVE PUBLICATIONS, P.O. Box 141, Bogota, New Jersey 07603-0141.

ISBN 0-9634306-4-6

Note: In some Scripture quotations, italics have been added by the author for emphasis only.

DEDICATIONS

Above all, I publicly recognize and honor my Heavenly Father for giving me life and salvation through Jesus Christ. I thank my parents, Joe and Jessie Howard for giving me birth.

May God bless all of you whose path crossed mine because in some way you have impacted my experiences. I compliment my son, Kwame, for being a model of support. This relationship has taught me patience and endurance. My relationship with my sisters, Joanne and Kathy and my brother, Aaron, exemplifies the true meaning of family. Thank you Atchafala, Debbie and Mayra for your demonstration of faithful support by your many prayers. I thank GiGi, Joan and Makaya for true love.

My relationship with my husband, Ron, has taught me steadfastness, perseverance and compassion. I dedicate the last chapter (God of Praise) of this book to him as we commit to spend the last chapter of our lives together.

If I didn't specifically mention your name, its not because I didn't think of you. You're included in the "all of you whose path crossed mine". Whether by friendship or hardship, your presence played some role in shaping my attitude. If it was by friendship, thank you. If it was by hardship, I used that to learn perseverance.

Of course, a revered thanks to the publisher of this book, End Time Wave Publications, for being "**in time**".

CONTENTS

PRAYER FOR SALVATION

For God so loved the world, that he gave his only begotten Son, that whosoever believeth in him should not perish, but have everlasting life.

John 3:16

Heavenly Father, forgive me for my sins. I believe that Jesus died on the cross, was wounded for my transgressions and bruised for my iniquities.I invite the Lord Jesus to come into my heart and to become the Lord over my life.

I accept the gift of your only begotten Son, Jesus Christ, so that I will have everlasting life. I confess with my mouth the Lord Jesus and believe in my heart that you raised him from the dead. I call upon the name of the Lord, therefore, I am saved.

INTRODUCTION

The effectual fervent prayer of a righteous man availeth much.

James 5:16

In most books, the Prayer for Salvation is placed at the end of the book, however, in this book the Prayer for Salvation is placed at the **beginning** and the **end**.

Immediately, you are faced with an urgent question. Are you Born Again? Have you accepted Jesus Christ into your heart?

Accepting Jesus Christ is the key that opens and unlocks the prayers contained in this book. He is the author of "**THE BOOK**", the great book of life. Is your name written in the Lamb's book of life?

Since you have picked-up this book, and at this very moment, it is in your possession, you are obviously concerned about your prayer life. Therefore, it seems only appropriate that you would want to ensure that there is nothing to hinder you receiving a fuller revelation of prayer. You will learn to love prayer and to increase and develop a prayer life far beyond anything you could ever imagine.

Jesus Christ is our salvation; the **Alpha** and **Omega,** the **beginning** and the **end**, the **first** and the **last.** The prayer at the beginning of the book signifies that Jesus Christ is the **Alpha**, the **beginning** and the

first. The prayer at the end of the book signifies that he is the **Omega**, the **end** and the **last.** The word of God is a finished work. It has been sealed by Jesus Christ.

Jesus Christ the same, yesterday, today and forever.

Hebrews 13:8

Prayer is giving God back His Word. He is faithful to His Word, and hastens to perform it. His Word does not return to Him void.

Before each prayer, there are illustrations to explain situations leading to the prayer. It is important to know why a particular kind of prayer is prayed. Each spoken Word, in prayer, has the power to become manifested in the natural world as long as you believe the spoken Word and pray by faith.

At the end of each prayer, there is a positive thought to keep in mind. Think on it until your prayer manifests. Your prayer came to life, in the spiritual world, the moment you spoke it. Think positive!

If you are not Born Again, pray the Prayer for Salvation, from your heart, so that you will become a child of God, and to fully receive and appreciate the words and blessings contained in this book. If you are Born Again, by reading the Prayer for Salvation, you will, hopefully, be reminded of the power within you and the victories that await you.

This book contains many prayers, but the most important prayer is the Prayer for Salvation.

PREFACE

Sometimes we have to be creative in our thinking so that our thoughts will become more like God's thoughts. So, imagine yourself carrying an empty bucket. One day you may need **blessings, deliverance** or **finances**. Another day, calls for **health,** a **home** or **love**. **Marriage** always requires attention. **Peace** reigns high on the throne. **Youth** stand in need of fervent prayer. Thank God for **praise**.

Whatever you need, God has it in abundance. Fill your bucket from His well. His well never runs dry, but is everlasting.

It has always been a part of my character to "get things done", and to use available power and resources. Having accomplished some of my goals, with God's might, I began to desire a closer walk with God, and to know His purpose and will. I prayed, earnestly, for him to show me and direct me.

Upon completion of the Christian Training Program at the church I attend, it's suggested to become a part of one of the Helps ministries. I searched the list of ministries, but none appealed to me. I asked God what ministry I should become a part of. I waited. His answer was very direct and powerful. He said: "**You have an enormous amount of power within you, but it's been misdirected. I'm going to redirect it to change the world, to influence people's lives and to impact nations."**

Naturally, amazement absorbed me as I

wondered, "How would I impact nations?" It sounded so awesome. As I waited upon the Lord, eventually, it became very clear that God wanted me to become a part of the Prayer Ministry at my church. **I would impact nations through prayer.** I was not totally surprised since I had already developed a love for prayer and had witnessed many answers to prayer.

My call to prayer began in November 1993. God instructed me to, "Listen to the Prophets." I was lead to read Jeremiah, Chapter 1. Verse ten refers to nations: "See, I have this day set thee over nations and over the kingdoms, to root out, and to pull down, and to destroy, and to throw down, to build, and to plant."

This call to prayer was further confirmed at my first attendance to Friday night prayer at church. Immediately, upon entering the sanctuary, the prayer leader was referencing Jeremiah, Chapter 1, in particular, Verse 10 regarding "nations".

God takes what we have and are willing to give him, and uses it to perfect the body of Christ. God took my character, "to get things done", in the natural, and used it **to get things done** in the spirit realm.

I have always had a passion for writing, especially poetry. Having accumulated quite a bit of poetry, I yearned to "do something with it" other than watch it collect dust.

A book entitled, "Understanding Your Potential" by Myles Munroe timely arrived in my hands. I hungrily digested its contents. The fire was really ignited upon reading: "Though it may surprise you, the richest deposits on our planet lie just a few blocks from your house. They rest in your local cemetery or graveyard. Buried beneath the soil within the walls of those sacred grounds are dreams that never came to pass, songs that were never sung, books that were never written, paintings that never filled a canvas, ideas that were never shared, visions that never became reality, inventions that were never designed, plans that never went beyond the drawing board of the mind and purposes that were never fulfilled. Our graveyards are filled with potential that remained potential."

I knew I had to share my writing, **or something**, with others. Again, God revealed **HIS** plan. It was not my poetry, but prayers. The seed was planted, and it took root on July 5, 1993 when my sister, Joanne, and her family, gave me a journal. Upon opening the journal, I immediately turned to a page with the Bible verse (Proverbs 16:3), "Commit to the Lord whatever you do, and your plans will succeed." Since that date, I became God's vessel to inspire you to develop a life of victory through prayer.

JACQUELYN BRYANT
APRIL1995

ACKNOWLEDGEMENTS

Thank you for sharing in the vision to impact nations through prayer. The gift which was sent from you "is an odor of a sweet smell, a sacrifice, acceptable and well pleasing to God" (Phil. 4:18).

Your barns shall be filled with plenty (Proverbs 3:10) and as you have watered, you shall be watered also (Proverbs 11:25).

****

Ronald J. Bryant
Theresa Brown - Roberts
Isabelle Cain
Mr. and Mrs. Willie Cain
Rev. and Mrs. John Dupree
Edith, Gwendolyn, Marilyn and Kenneth Ford
Dec. William Franklin
Janice L. Gloster, Ph.D.
Aaron R. Howard
Jessie M. Howard
Thelma K. Howard
B. Joanne Jackson
Khari A. Jackson
Makaya J. Jackson
Maree's Hair Keez
Kwame F. King
Librada Mesa
Rev. Charles and Emily Primm
Eileen Quirk
Estella Williams
In Memory of Hakeema (Toy) Majeed and
Donna (Najiyyah) Johnson

CHAPTER 1

GOD OF BLESSINGS

. ..if I will not open you the windows of heaven and pour you out a blessing that there shall not be room enough to receive it.

Malachi 3:10

Our Heavenly Father is blessed beyond anything we can ever imagine. It is His nature and character. The human mind can not even come close to perceiving the magnitude of our **blessed** Creator.

Try to imagine the power and resources required to create a heaven, an earth and man. I believe our minds would burst out of order if we spend too much time and thought attempting to perceive such a challenge. Therefore, let's accept the fact that power and resources beyond and above our finite imagination went into the creation of heaven, earth and man.

Even today, with all of our superior technology and all of the scholarly opportunities and advancement, man can never come close to the knowledge and power of Almighty God, or even begin to understand His majestic nature.

Isaiah 55:8 and 9 tells us that God's thoughts and ways are not like ours, but His ways and thoughts are higher than the heavens are above the earth.

Yes, our Heavenly Father is blessed abundantly. Abundantly is defined as: marked by great plenty, abounding, a degree of plentifulness. My favorite definition of blessed is: to confer prosperity or happiness upon, bringing pleasure or contentment. However, these definitions can merely define the abundance of God's blessedness. God is a blessing.

When someone is blessed in such a great magnitude, there has to be an overflow, an outpouring of such. So, obviously, there must be a vessel to receive the overflow. **The children of God is that vessel.** Hallelujah!

I experienced a memorable moment with my Heavenly Father while attending a Christian retreat in the Pennsylvania mountains.

It was mid-winter. Snow and ice were on the ground. Freshly fallen snow covered the bare tree limbs and the surrounding mountains. Water was running down a rocky trail. I wondered where the water was coming from. My curiosity persuaded me to search for the source of that water.

It was Sunday, the last day of my three-day retreat. I was determined that before I left I was going to find the source from which this water flowed. I noticed a walkway leading uphill. That morning at about 7:00 A.M., I started my journey. As I got farther uphill, I knew I was getting closer to my destination because the flow of the water was becoming more powerful.

Finally, I reached the source of the water. It was a vibrant and fascinating lake. It was covered with patches of ice. However, the patches of ice could not stop the water from gushing over the lake's brim. The power of the water was unceasing even under such adverse circumstances. The power and energy of the flow of the water amazed me.

I began my journey downhill. I noticed that the flow of water was becoming less powerful and was losing its force as it got farther away from its source. As I reached the bottom of the hill, the water was very weak and powerless.

At that moment, God gave me an intense revelation. He said, "Notice that the water lost its power and strength as it drew farther from the lake, which is its source. Stay close to me. I am your source. The closer you stay to me, the more powerful you will be. If you move away from me, you will have less power and strength. You will become weak."

The water represents the living Word of God. Jesus states in John 4:14 that if you drink of this water, you will never thirst again because this water is a well springing up into everlasting life.

Every time the water gushed out of the lake, it carried a blessing. The children of God are the vessel for God's power, strength, love, mercy, and grace. All that he is; we are.

Jesus pronounces an abundance of blessings in the Beatitudes: *Blessed are the poor in spirit, they that mourn, the meek, those that hunger and thirst after righteousness, the merciful, the pure in heart, the peacemakers and the persecuted.* This is surely a demonstration of an overflow of God's blessings.

Luke 6:38 says: *Give and it shall be given, pressed down, shaken together and running over.* God is the giver. All of His blessings are pressed down, shaken together and running over. His name is synonymous with blessed, giver and creator.

Stay close to God. He is your source of power and strength.

> **But they that wait upon the Lord shall renew their strength; they shall mount up with wings as eagles; they shall run, and not be weary; and they shall walk, and not faint.**
>
> **Isaiah 40:31**

Just as the eagle mounts up, be at the top of the mountain so that you will be close to your source. You will be blessed abundantly. According to John 10:10, Jesus states, "I am come that they might have life, and that they might have it more abundantly."

Malachi 3:10 says God will pour out blessings. However, prior to the pouring, there is an act on your part to bring all your tithes into His storehouse. Your blessings hinges on your obedience. You must know the Word of God and the will of God. Hosea 4:6 says, "My people are destroyed for lack of knowledge."

Abraham was blessed because of his obedience. God told him to go to an unknown land, leaving behind everything familiar. He set himself up to receive the blessings poured out from the windows of heaven.

Blessings are always present because God is always present. Whatever the circumstances are in your life, there is a corresponding blessing. Don't allow disobedience and a lack of knowledge of God's Word hinder your blessings. You are God's vessel.

Prayer for Blessings: Heavenly Father, I acknowledge you as a mighty blessed God, full of overflowing blessings. When you pour out blessings, I want to be in the right place to receive them. I don't want anything in my life to be a hindrance. I want to know your Word and your will for my life. Your Word is a lamp unto my feet and a light unto my path. It is life to me and health to my flesh.

You said to prove you, the windows of Heaven would open and blessings would pour out. You honor your Word, therefore, the proof is in your faithfulness to your Word alone. Your Word does not return to you void, but accomplishes what it is sent to accomplish and prospers where it is sent. It shall bring forth buds, give seed to the sower and bread to the eater.

Jesus came so that I would have an abundant life. He blesses the poor in spirit, giving them the kingdom of heaven. He comforts those that mourn, and promises that the meek inherits the earth. Those that hunger and thirst after righteousness shall be filled. The merciful shall obtain mercy and the pure in heart shall see God. The peacemakers shall be called the children of God. The kingdom of Heaven is reserved for those persecuted for righteousness' sake.

I will look upon the fowls of the air and how you feed them, and consider the lilies of the field and how they grow. Therefore, I will take no thought for tomorrow by worrying or being anxious because you will provide all of my needs according to your riches in glory by Christ Jesus, In Jesus' name. Amen.

Think on these things: God is my source. I am His vessel.

CHAPTER 2

GOD OF DELIVERANCE

For the eyes of the Lord run to and fro throughout the whole earth, to shew himself strong in the behalf of them whose heart is perfect toward him.

II Chronicles, 16:9

Joseph dreamed of being exalted and having obeisance given to him. He revealed these dreams to his brothers who immediately hardened their hearts against him and became jealous. His brothers developed a wicked plot to take his life. Joseph became a victim of hate, envy, conspiracy, lies and cruelty. His older brother, Reuben, interceded because he did not want to see his brother killed. Instead Joseph was sold for twenty pieces of silver. Unknowingly, the wicked plot devised by Joseph's brothers resulted in good. In Genesis 50:20, Joseph speaks to his brothers: "Ye thought evil against me; but God meant it unto good."

Genesis 39:1-6 tells all of the victories that God **caused** to come upon Joseph. He became a prosperous man. The Lord **made** all that he did to prosper in his hand. He found favor in the sight of his master. He became the overseer of his master's possessions. God **caused** Joseph to be fruitful in the land of his affliction (Genesis 41:52). The Lord even blessed the master's house for Joseph's sake. Hallelujah!

What trials are you facing today? Are you prepared for the trials and tests of tomorrow? The Word of God tells us to put on the whole armor of God so that we will be able to stand in the evil day.

Be prepared! We are warned in I Peter 4:12, "Beloved, think it not strange concerning the fiery trial which **is** to try you..." To prepare for the fiery trials, know the Word of God and use it in effective prayer. Ephesians 6:12 tells us that we wrestle not against flesh and blood, but against principalities, against powers, against the rulers of the darkness of this world, against spiritual wickedness in high places. Prayer is our weapon against principalities, powers, rulers of darkness, and spiritual wickedness in high places. We need spiritual warfare to combat them. Since these things are occurring in the spirit realm, we need to use **like** weapons, "For the weapons of our warfare are not carnal..." (II Corinthians 10:4). In other words our weapons must be of a compatible nature: spiritual against spiritual when combating in the spirit realm; physical against physical when combating in the natural realm.

The Lord is my rock, and my fortress, and my deliverer; my God, my strength, in whom I will trust; my buckler, and the horn of my salvation, and my high tower.

Psalm 18:2

Prayer for Deliverance: Heavenly Father, I acknowledge you as my deliverer, therefore, I am victoriously saved from every evil plot set against me. Every plot set against me is a weapon. It is written, according to your Word, that no weapon formed against me shall prosper. I confess with my mouth and believe in my heart that (insert specific situation) which was meant for evil, you will turn it around for good.

I fear no evil because you are with me. I dwell in the secret place of the most High and abide under the shadow of the Almighty. You are a mountain and a wall of fire round about me. You are my refuge and strength, a very present help in trouble.

Allow me to find grace and mercy in the sight of all of those necessary to aid in my victory. I put my trust in you; my rock, my fortress and my deliverer. Give your angels charge over me to keep me in all of my ways. Thank you for satisfying me with peace and long life, in Jesus' name. Amen.

Think on these things: Just as Joseph was delivered, God will also deliver me.

CHAPTER 3

GOD OF FINANCES

> **And I will make of thee a great nation, and I will bless thee, and make thy name great; and thou shalt be a blessing: And I will bless them that bless thee, and curse him that curseth thee; and in thee shall all families of the earth be blessed.**
>
> **Genesis 12:2-3**

All families of the earth shall be blessed. Are you a part of God's family here on the earth? If you can answer "Yes" to this question, you are blessed. If you have accepted Jesus Christ as your Lord and Savior, you are Abraham's seed. All of the blessings that God promised Abraham are yours. You have inherited them.

Many people are content with their financial status only because they don't believe they have the power within them to change it. You have the power to make a change. You have the power to tread on serpents, scorpions and over all the power of the enemy (Luke 10:19). God has given you a spirit of power.

Well, why am I so poor? Why am I living from paycheck to paycheck? Either you don't know the promises of God, you have chosen not to believe them, or your actions have prevented them from coming alive.

If I'm Abraham's seed and of the family of God why is there so much lack in my life. If you used the Word "**if**", you are obviously in doubt, lack faith and don't believe God's promises. You have to substitute the "**if**" for an "**I AM**". You have to fully believe that **YOU ARE** in the family of God and that your inheritance is your right.

God proclaimed in Exodus 3:14: "**I AM THAT I AM**" and tell them that "**I AM**" sent you. He displayed faith and belief in who he was and is. You too must believe to the point when you can boldly confess, without doubt: **I am** in the family of God. When you can do this, you are well on your way towards your goal; effective prayer and overwhelming blessings.

You must display that same authority in proclaiming that you are the blessed seed of Abraham and a part of God's family.

Get rid of the "if" word. Satan used the word "if" to challenge Jesus (Matthew 4:3-9). Satan knew, without any doubt, that Jesus was the son of God. However, he used the word "if" hoping to intimidate Jesus, cast doubt and cause Jesus to lose faith. It didn't work for Jesus, and it doesn't have to work for you. Remove "if" from your vocabulary. Replace it with "faith".

The Word of God tells us that we must hearken diligently unto His voice, observe and do all His commandments (Deuteronomy 28:1). God is very specific in the area concerning finances. There is no doubt that he was referring to tangible blessings in Deuteronomy 28. Verse 8 tells us that the Lord **shall command** the blessing upon thee in thy storehouses. Verse eleven tells us that the Lord **shall make** thee plenteous in goods because of His promise.

Proverbs 8:17-21 speaks of **durable** riches. His fruit is better than fine gold and His revenue is better than choice silver.

> **That I may cause those that love me to inherit substance; and I will fill their treasures.**
>
> **Proverbs 8:21**

God wants to cause you to inherit these promises. He spoke to Isaac, Abraham's son, and told him that he would perform the oath that he had sworn unto Abraham because Abraham obeyed his voice and kept his commandments. Isaac received his inheritance and was blessed because of Abraham's obedience, and most importantly, because God made an oath. Proof of God's faithfulness to His Word can be found in Genesis 26:12; Isaac sowed and received a hundredfold, and the Lord blessed him. God is always faithful to His Word. Since God is faithful to His Word, we must be faithful to His Word, also.

We are encouraged in the Word of God to prove His faithfulness. Malachi 3:10 tells us "Prove me now herewith, saith the Lord of host, if I will not open you the windows of heaven, and pour you out a blessing that there shall not be room enough to receive it."

Because of Abraham's obedience and faith, God was faithful to His Word. Abraham was **very** rich in cattle, silver and gold. All of these are durable riches as mentioned in Proverbs 8:18. Abraham was not just rich, but the words **"very rich"** are emphasized in Genesis 13:2. As a matter of fact, Abraham and his nephew, Lot, had so many riches and possessions between them, they could no longer dwell together in the same land. Their substance was so great they had to separate.

You might ask, how did this come to pass? How was God able to do this? Can God do this for me, today? The answer to these questions can be found in knowing God's divine ownership.

The heavens are thine, the earth also is thine: as for the world and the fullness thereof, thou has founded them.

Psalm 89:11

Abraham was very rich in **cattle**, **silver** and **gold**. Why? Because everything belongs to God.

For every beast of the forest is mine, and the cattle upon a thousand hills.

Psalm 50:10

The silver is mine, and the gold is mine, saith the Lord of hosts.

Haggai 2:8

Everything that Abraham was very rich in belonged to God; cattle, silver and gold.

What must you do to receive your inheritance?

- Accept Jesus as your Lord and Savior to become a member of God's family. (Pray from your heart, in faith, the prayer in the beginning of this book.)

- Tithe: Malachi 3:7-12 cautions us against robbing God, and encourages us to bring **all** of our tithes into the storehouse.

Learn and **love** to bring all your tithes into the storehouse. Do not rob God! The key that released the blessings upon Abraham was his obedience. He hearkened diligently unto the voice of God and kept **His** commandments, statutes and ordinances. Tithing is an ordinance of God (Malachi 3:7).

Give with a cheerful and willing heart. The Israelites were so willing in their hearts to give for the building of the tabernacle that they gave more than enough (Genesis 36:3-7). They were asked to cease from giving. Now, that's evidence of a willing heart to give.

Your part is to open the door: be obedient, acknowledge your inheritance and receive it by faith. Call those things that be not as though they were.

What financial crisis are you facing today? Do you need finances for your children's education, rent, mortgage, over-due bills? Perhaps you're not facing a financial crisis at all, but simply want to receive your rightful inheritance.

And if ye be Christ's then are ye Abraham's seed, and heirs according to the promise.

Galatians 3:29

All of the mentioned scriptures point to the fact that **God owns everything** which includes our personal finances. We don't own anything! Everything belongs to God! He entrusts His goods to us as stewards.

The story in Luke 16:1-13 describes the steward who was called upon to give an account of his stewardship.

Since we own nothing, the most we can do is to ask God for wisdom in the use and the disbursement of what is His. Any unwise choices that we make, can cause financial need and lack in the area of our finances. In other words, we will surely reap the fruit of our labor.

Prayer for Finances: Heavenly Father, I confess those things that I have done to contribute to any financial need or lack by not being a good steward. I pray for wisdom to be diligent in my finances and the choices that I must make.

Thank you, Heavenly Father, for revealing your Word to me and taking me out of darkness into light so that I can be blessed in my finances and in all durable goods. I shall not want or need of any good thing because it is written that the Lord shall **give** that which is good, and will supply all of my needs according to His riches in glory by Christ Jesus. The earth is yours and the fullness thereof. Therefore, I command that all of the blessings come upon me and overtake me according to your Word. By this prayer, your faithfulness to your Word and my diligence in keeping your commandments, the windows of heaven are open.

I pray that you will cause a mighty host of angels to go forth, on my behalf, to hasten to perform your Word. Abraham obeyed your voice and kept your charge, commandments, statues and laws, and I am Abraham's seed. You said in your Word that you would perform the oath you swore unto Abraham that all of the families of the earth shall be blessed.

I desire my inheritance (or specific need). I believe that I receive it, therefore, I shall have it. I delight myself in you knowing that you will give me the desires of my heart.

I loose the powers necessary to bring my inheritance (or specific need) to me in Jesus' name.

Amen.

Think on these things: I want to be a lender not a borrower and a blessing to others.

CHAPTER 4

GOD OF HEALTH

> **For I will restore health unto thee, and I will heal thee of thy wounds, saith the Lord...**
>
> **Jeremiah 30:17**

Matthew 9:18 tells a story about Jairus' daughter whose life was restored because of the earth-moving faith her father had in the Word of God, Jesus' healing power.

> **...My daughter is even now dead: but come and lay thy hand upon her, and she shall live.**
>
> **Matthew 9:18**

Jairus admitted to Jesus, in Matthew 9:18, that his daughter was dead. His next words exemplified his faith; "but come and lay thy hand upon her, and she shall live."

Jairus' attitude was; my daughter's restoration of life is possible when Jesus lay His hand upon her, and I expect it.

He knew that once Jesus laid his hand upon his daughter, her life would be restored. This is what he believed, expected and received.

A DEFINITION OF FAITH: FAITH IS WHAT YOU BELIEVE IS POSSIBLE WITH GOD AND YOU EXPECT IT.

Therefore I say unto you, What things soever ye desire, when ye pray, believe that ye receive them, and ye shall have them.

Mark 11:24

Jesus responded to Jairus' level of faith and his attitude towards Jesus' touch.

And Jesus arose, and followed him, and so did his disciples.

Matthew 9:19

Jairus **believed,** and Jesus **moved** on what Jairus believed and expected.

The words "**arose**", "**believed**" and "**moved**" are all action words. Jairus started the action; he **believed**. As a result of his belief; Jesus took action, he **arose** and followed Jairus.

Jesus arose and restored the life of Jairus' daughter. However, the ultimate ascension was when Jesus arose according to I Peter 3:22.

Who is gone into heaven, and is on the right hand of God; angels and authorities and powers being made subject unto him.

I Peter 3:22

This time His resurrection didn't just restore one life, as in Jairus' story, but he **OVERCAME** death and provided eternal life for all humanity. Jesus Christ is our risen Savior. Hallelujah!

For the wages of sin is death; but the gift of God is eternal life through Jesus Christ our Lord.

Romans 6:23

Another miraculous healing occured with the woman with the issue of blood. She was healed instantly upon touching Jesus' garment. She believed that a touch of His garment would heal her.

For she said within herself, If I may but touch his garment, I shall be whole.

Matthew 9:21

She was healed because of what she believed and expected; to touch Jesus' garment. The key to this miracle was her faith in touching His garment.

Matthew 9:27 tells a story about two blind men whose faith was in the mercy of Jesus.

...two blind men followed him, crying, and saying, Thou son of David, have mercy on us.

Matthew 9:27

The two blind men could have said, "We are blind, give us sight," but they chose to say, "have mercy." Their eyes were opened because Jesus had mercy on them according to what they believed and expected.

The key to this miracle was "have mercy." They believed in Jesus' mercy.

But God, who is rich in mercy, for his great love wherewith he loved us.

Ephesians 2:4

These three miracles occured as a result of three different beliefs of expectation: laying on of hands, a touch of a garment and Jesus' mercy. **All three were founded on faith**. They all had different beliefs, but they demonstrated great faith in the power of Almighty God.

Miracles still occur today. However, it's not necessary for Jesus to lay hands on us, or to touch His garment. Thank God that His mercy endures forever.

O give thanks unto the Lord; for he is good; for his mercy endureth for ever.

I Chronicles 16:34

In all three illustrations, the expected occured as a result of Jesus' physical presence. However, Mark 11:22-24 encourages us, today, to have faith in God, move mountains, what we say shall come to pass and what we believe, we will receive.

When Jesus was crucified on the cross, he bore all of our sins.

But he was wounded for our transgressions, bruised for our iniquities: the chastisement of our peace was upon him; and with his stripes we are healed.

Isaiah 53:5

The word "**transgression**" is defined as a violation of a law, command or duty. The word "**iniquity**" is defined as wickedness or sin. Upon reading these definitions, our thoughts may become dismal. The same thoughts occur when we think of sickness and disease. **However, the words of Isaiah, 53:5, should make us realize our victory and proclaim joy.**

A merry heart doeth good like a medicine...

Proverbs 17:22

The word "**peace**" is defined as a state of tranquillity, harmony or quiet. The word "**healed**" is defined as to make sound or whole; to restore to health; to restore to original purity or integrity; to return to a sound state.

There are many miraculous healings mentioned in the New Testament.

The most important verse in the Bible that lets us know that healing and divine health are ours is John 1:1 "In the beginning was the Word, and the Word was with God, and the Word was God." John 1 verses 4 and 5 tells us that **in him was life which is the light of men and the light shines in darkness.**

Sickness and disease is darkness, but the light, which is life, shines in darkness. Since the light shines in darkness, there should be no sickness. Light and dark can not occupy the same space. There is such a distinct difference between light and dark that God divided the light from the darkness according to Genesis 1:4. **God saw the light and it was good.**

Proverbs 4:20 cautions us to heed God's Word: "My son, attend to my **words**; incline thine ear unto my sayings." John 1:1 emphasizes that Jesus Christ is the Word.

In many of the instances of healing, Jesus' physical presence was there when the healing occured. Today, His presence is represented by the Word (John 1:1). We must speak the word and have faith in the Word to be healed.

Proverbs 4:21 urges us not to let the words depart from our eyes and to keep the Word in the midst of our hearts.

> **For they are life unto those that find them, and health to all their flesh.**
>
> **Proverbs 4:22**

Notice the interchange between Jesus and the Word. His presence healed in the past, the Word heals today. We can say I was healed by Jesus Christ, or we can say, I was healed by the Word of God.

If sickness or disease, which is darkness, enters into the body, the body becomes dark. Nothing should invade our bodies that prevents us from exemplifying that we are created in the image of God.

And God said, Let us make man in our image, after our likeness...

Genesis 1:26

How is light restored? How is the sickness removed? Ephesians 6:11-17 tells us all we need to restore light and shed darkness.

Put on the whole armour of God, that ye may be able to stand against the wiles of the devil.

Ephesians 6:11

Picture your body as a house. Your head is the roof. Take on the helmet of salvation. Your feet is the foundation of the house. Clothe your feet with the preparation of the gospel of peace.

In between your head and feet, the roof and the foundation, are all of the other rooms of the house which represents your various body parts; heart, lungs, legs and so on. According to Ephesians 6:13-17, all of the body parts have protection: they are protected with truth, the breastplate of righteousness, the sword of the Spirit, which is the Word of God, and **above all is the shield of faith**. The armor is the Word of God.

And the prayer of faith shall save the sick, and the Lord shall raise him up...

James 5:15

Prayer for Health: Heavenly Father, I command that this sickness (say specific name, if known) be uprooted and loose my body right now in the sovereign-almighty name of Jesus Christ. No weapon formed against my body shall prosper. Your Word in me forms a mighty bolt of lightning to cancel and destroy the assignment of any sickness or disease.

My body will not serve two masters. I choose to serve Jesus Christ only. I present my body to you as a living sacrifice, holy and acceptable which is my reasonable service, according to your Word.

My body has been sanctified and cleansed with the washing of your Word so that it may be presented to Christ as a glorious church without spot, wrinkle or blemish.

I thank you that your Word is life to me and health to my flesh. No sickness or disease can dwell in my body because Jesus Christ dwells within.

By the stripes of Jesus, I am healed, in Jesus's name. Amen

Think on these things: I believe it! I expect it!

CHAPTER 5

GOD OF HOMES

> **Through wisdom is an house builded; and by understanding it is established: And by knowledge shall the chambers be filled with all precious and pleasant riches.**
>
> **Proverbs 24:3-4**

God wants our homes to be built through wisdom and filled with **precious** and **pleasant** riches. The word precious is defined as something of great value, highly esteemed and cherished, excessively refined. The word pleasant is defined as having qualities that render pleasure, and an agreeable nature. These qualities are not always evident in most homes because homes are being built by man instead of being built by God, Jehovah Shalom.

> **Except the Lord build the house, they labour in vain that build it: except the Lord keep the city, the watchman waketh but in vain.**
>
> **Psalm 127:1**

Hezekiah was very sick. He was warned of the prophet Isaiah to set his house in order because he was going to die (Isaiah 38:1). He immediately heeded this warning, turned his face to God and prayed (Isaiah 38:2-3).

God honored Hezekiah's prayer. The Lord spoke to Isaiah again, but this time he instructed him to tell Hezekiah that he had heard his prayer, seen his tears and would add fifteen years to his life (Isaiah 38:4-5).

What an astounding response to prayer. God heard, saw and responded. Relate this warning to your own home, your dwelling place. Is your house in order?

To set your house in order, proclaim that you and everyone in your house will serve the Lord just as Joshua proclaimed in chapter 24, verse 15, "...as for me and my house, we **will** serve the Lord." Dedicate your house to the Lord. Commit everyone and everything in your house to the Lord.

Commit thy works unto the Lord, and thy thoughts shall be established.

Proverbs 16:3

Has your dwelling place become a place of **dry bones**? Speak life over your dwelling place.

The Spirit of the Lord lead Ezekiel to a valley full of dry bones. The Lord told Ezekiel to speak to the bones and tell them to hear the Word of the Lord (Ezekiel 37:1-4).

Thus saith the Lord God unto these bones; Behold, I will cause breath to enter into you, and ye shall live.

Ezekiel 37:5

The bones came together and flesh covered them. Then God commanded Ezekiel to prophesy to the wind to breathe upon the bones the breath of life.

So I prophesied as he commanded me, and the breath

came into them, and they lived, and stood up upon their feet, and exceeding great army.

Ezekiel 37:10

Has the fountain in your dwelling place become dry?

I will open rivers in high places, and fountains in the midst of the valleys: I will make the wilderness a pool of water, and the dry land springs of water.

Isaiah 41:18

Isaiah 49:10 tells us that springs of water shall guide us. Everyone who thirst, drink of the waters (Isaiah 55:1).

Your dwelling place is your home, your abode, and should be your place of refuge and fortress. It should render pleasure and those abiding within, should be of an agreeable nature.

Prayer for Homes: Thank you, Heavenly Father, for being our dwelling place, our abode, our refuge and our fortress. We dedicate our home to you so it will be everything you are to us: a place of refuge and a fortress where peace reigns and an agreeable nature exists.

Build our house Lord. Set it in order so that our dwelling place will be of great value, highly esteemed and cherished. Refine us so that we will be on one accord and of the same spirit, the spirit of the Lord. We will speak the same thing, the living Word of God, and we will be perfectly joined together in the same mind, the mind of Christ.

Cause breath to enter into the dry places and fountains in the midst of the valleys.

Make our home a fortress and all abiding within an exceeding great army to stand against every fiery trial and temptation.

The demonstration of your love, allows Christ to dwell in us. We know and believe your love. Your Word says that you are love and he that dwells in love, dwells in God, and God in him. Thank you for being our dwelling place, in Jesus' name. Amen.

Think on these things: The foundation of my home is the Rock.

CHAPTER 6

GOD OF LOVE

Nor height, nor depth, nor any other creature, shall be able to separate us from the love of God, which is in Christ Jesus our Lord.

Romans 8:39

Genuine love will allow you to love others unconditionally and to accept yourself, as well. In order to love anyone else, you must first love yourself. You must first accept yourself, unconditionally, then you can love others, unconditionally.

God is love. He demonstrated His love when he came to earth in the body of Jesus who died for us: What a sacrifice!

When we accept Jesus Christ as our Lord, we are accepting God's unconditional sacrifice; no strings attached. It is a great and precious **gift**.

For God so loved the world, that he gave his only begotten Son, that whosoever believeth in him should not perish, but have everlasting life.

John 3:16

God's love becomes our foundation. It is the only solid foundation we will ever have. Nothing can compete with it, or come close to it. Sure, there will be counterfeits of love, but once they are tried by the trials of life and every day occurrences, they will never stand the test. The fact that they are counterfeits will always be exposed.

God's love is eternal, therefore, it has a lasting effect upon our lives and in the things that we do and connect ourselves to. Without this love, we will never be totally committed to anything. Every characteristic that we have originates from God.
The character of commitment will be a missing element in our lives without God's eternal love.

God's love brings many aspects into our lives because of its many characteristics.

The Word of God, speaks of being fitly joined together in the body of Christ to increase the body and edify it in love (Ephesians 4:15-16).

Think of the body of Christ as a large puzzle that God plays with. Think of it as God's toy. He works on it daily. We are the individual pieces of the puzzle. As we submit our lives to Him, He picks us up in His hands and immediately begins to mold us and shape us so that we can fit into the puzzle. He purges and refines. We have to be pliable and willingly submit. The puzzle is God's plan and His will.

The Lord is a refiner and purifier of silver. He purges as gold that we may offer unto him an offering in righteousness (Malachi 3:2-3).

When he's finished with us, it will be the season

and the acceptable time. He will place us within the puzzle so that we fitly join with the other pieces already in place. The body of Christ will be more effective and powerful as it grows towards perfection.

> **And believers were the more added to the Lord, multitudes both of men and women.**
>
> **Acts 5:14**

Where God finally places us, will become the thing we will joyfully commit ourselves to. We will no longer have to search because we will know the will of God for our lives. We will have discovered our talents and gifts. We will be fulfilled and experience peace, contentment and happiness like never before. We will have found our place in life, the body of Christ. The body of Christ is life; everything outside of the body of Christ is dead. God is life.

Have your adventures and personal pursuits become meaningless? Are you experiencing emptiness and void? Are you always searching for fulfillment? Have you begin to question life and its purpose?

Searching and questioning, in some instances, lead to drugs, alcohol, lasciviousness and other vices which will eventually lead to destruction rather than fulfillment.

A couple of years ago, I experienced emptiness and void. I began to pray and question my purpose in life.

Rather than take on unhealthy vices, I began to study the book of Ecclesiastes. After all, I reasoned, why should I waste my time and jeopardize my health trying things that may or may not be the answer when Solomon had already taken on this venture.

Solomon reveals the unsatisfied state of man in Ecclesiastes 1:8, "...the eye is not satisfied with seeing, nor the ear filled with hearing". Verses 5-7 reveals that there is even a restlessness in the things of nature; the sun, the wind, the rivers and the sea are all in a state of flux.

> **He gave his heart to seek and search out, by wisdom, all things under the sun**
>
> **I have seen all the works that are done under the sun; and behold, all is vanity and vexation of spirit.**
>
> **Ecclesiastes 1:14**

The second chapter of Ecclesiastes reveals that Solomon took on every imaginable vice and venture. He sought pleasure, wine and folly. He planted vineyards, got servants, maidens and great possessions. He withheld nothing from himself.

> **And whatsoever mine eyes desired I kept not from them, I withheld not my heart from any joy...**
>
> **Ecclesiastes 2:10**

However, after each pursuit, he continued to return to the same conclusion; that all was vanity and vexation of spirit.

There are close to 40 mentions of the word "I" in Chapter two of Ecclesiastes. This attests to the egotistical attitude of human beings; the "I" syndrome which often leads to despair and emptiness.

Solomon finally concludes, with determination, that everything is vanity accept keeping the commandments of God, which is our duty.

> **Let us hear the conclusion of the whole matter: fear God, and keep his commandments: for this is the whole duty of man.**
>
> **Ecclesiastes 12:13**

What are the commandments of God? Jesus answered this question in Matthew 22:36-40 when questioned by one of the Pharisees, who was a lawyer.

> **Jesus said unto him, Thou shalt love the Lord thy God with all thy heart, and with all thy soul, and with all thy mind. This is the first and great commandment. And the second is like unto it, Thou shalt love they neighbor as thyself. On these two commandments hang all the law and the prophets.**
>
> **Matthew 22: 37-40**

It is clear that everything in life hinges on these two great commandments. These two commandments are the truths which takes us out of darkness into God's magnificent light. God's light is His love which conquers all. It fulfills our emptiness, it contents our discontent, and ceases our searches.

Evidence of obeying God's great commandments is demonstrated in devoting our lives to God and loving our neighbors as ourselves. His commandments are not grievous.

> **By this we know that we love the children of God, when we love God, and keep his commandments. For this is the love of God, that we keep his commandments; and his commandments are not grievous.**
>
> **I John 5: 2-3**

GOD'S LOVE PROVIDES:

Eyes to see (Psalms 119:37)
Ears to hear (Isaiah 30:21)
Guides the work of our hands (Ecclesiastes (9:10)
Controls our tongues (Psalms 35:28)
Orders our footsteps (Psalms 37:23)
Gives us life and health (Proverbs 4:22)
Protects our hearts and minds (Philippians 4:7)
Gives us positive thoughts (Philippians 4:8)
Replaces mourning with joy and heaviness with praise (Isaiah 61:3)

When you have entered into that place where you allow God the freedom to purify and refine you, you become more like Jesus, His child. When you allow God to teach, train, provide for, and nurture you, he becomes your Abba Father. You are no longer an orphan, but have been adopted into the family of God.

...but ye have received the Spirit of adoption, whereby we cry, Abba Father.

Romans 8:15

Because of His love sacrifice. His son Jesus, we are no longer under the law, we are no longer servants, but are sons and daughters. We can rightfully acknowledge God as our Abba Father. Hallelujah!

...God hath sent forth the Spirit of his Son into your hearts, crying, Abba Father...

Galatians 4:4-7

Jesus acknowledges God as "Abba Father" in His prayer; Mark 14:36. Jesus is our perfect example.

Prayer for Love: Abba Father, my desire is to be obedient to your commandments; to love the Lord my God with all my heart, soul and mind and to love my neighbor as myself.

I yield and submit myself to you to be pliable for you to purify and refine me as gold so that I keep your commandments and fitly join together in the body of Christ.

As you purify and refine me, I pray that my talents and gifts will come to life so that I may edify the body of Christ by giving back to you what you have placed in me. Because of your steadfast love for me, I will not be tossed to and fro, but will be grounded and rooted in you. Nothing shall separate me from your love. Because of your unchanging love, when I walk through the fire I will not be burned, your love will strengthen me, help me and uphold me with your righteousness.

Your love produces the fruit of the Spirit in my life and is a lamp unto my feet and a light unto my path. Your love makes the crooked paths straight, delivers me from temptation and leads me into green pastures, still waters and restores my soul.

Thank you that length of days, long life and peace shall be added unto me, in Jesus's name. Amen.

Think of these things: God's steadfast love.

In the beginning was the Word, and the Word was with God, and the Word was God.

John 1:1

CHAPTER 7

GOD OF MARRIAGE

Therefore shall a man leave his father and his mother, and shall cleave unto his wife: and they shall be one flesh.

Genesis 2:24

Genuine love is the substance that sustains a marriage. Genuine love is real, pure and authentic. You can see it, feel it and taste it. It has a character of its own. Genuine love can not be perfected in a mere physical attraction between man and woman.

Genuine love is attainable. However, it is not the same as perfect love. Perfect love is demonstrated in the love God has for us. Human love can be genuine but not perfect. Only God's love is perfect, flawless, and lacking nothing.

Nor height, nor depth, nor any other creature, shall be able to separate us from the love of God, which is in Christ Jesus our Lord.

Romans 8:39

For God so loved the world, that he gave his only begotten Son, that whosoever believeth in him should not perish, but have everlasting life.

John 3:16

There are many extraordinary love stories in the Bible that exceed that of Shakespeare's Romeo and Juliet.

For instance, an exciting love story is revealed in Genesis 24. Isaac never saw his bride, Rebekah. She was hand-picked by God. She served an important need in Isaac's life. She was a comfort to him after his mother, Sarah's death. Rebekah met Isaac's psychological need. God knew Isaac needed comfort after his mother's death.

Isaac was obedient to his father's oath of not wedding a Canaanite wife. Because of his obedience, God blessed him with the wife he required to fulfill his need.

Another vivid display of notable love is revealed in Genesis 29. Like father, like son, Jacob was obedient to his father Isaac's command that he too not marry a wife of the daughters of Canaan (Genesis 28:1). Because of his obedience, God also blessed him with Rachel, the wife he needed.

Jacob was enthralled by Rachel's beauty and fell in love with her immediately. He agreed to serve seven years in order for her to become his bride. However, he actually served a total of twenty years (Genesis 31:41). He was not just attracted to her physical beauty, but there was an intense spiritual attraction which becomes obvious as the entire love story is read. Rachel's beauty went far beyond physical beauty. Her inner person; the beauty of her spirit also attracted Jacob. He had to have been attracted to more than her outer beauty because he served many years beyond the initial seven years agreed to with her father. However, those year seemed only a few days to him (Genesis 29:20).

God knew that Jacob would serve many years for his bride. A solely physical attraction would not have endured the task of serving so many years.

In both instances, Isaac and Jacob were blessed in their helpmates because of their obedience.

A complete opposite image of love is illustrated in Judges 14. Verse one reveals that Samson **saw** a woman. She was apparently arousing, attractive and appealing to the eye because he told his parents, "I have **seen** a woman...now therefore get her for me to wife." In verse three he demands of his parents, "Get her for me; for she pleaseth me well." The attraction that Samson had for this woman, Delilah, was a physical attraction. He was so spellbound by her beauty and her luring spirit that he was completely oblivious to her cunning and subtle schemes to determine the source of his strength.

In each of these three impressive love stories, three very distinct circumstances can be observed.

First, Isaac had a tremendous need that Rebekah met. He needed comfort after his mother's death. He loved Rebekah for providing and fulfilling that need. He obviously missed his mother very much because he was in mental and emotional anguish. He needed Rebekah to fill the void. His frame of mind was obviously important and significant to know about since God made a point of putting it in the Bible. If it was not a significant issue, it would not be mentioned.

All scripture is given by inspiration of God, and is profitable for doctrine, for reproof, for correction, for instruction, in righteousness.

II Timothy 3:16

Rebekah's timely presence into Isaac's life allowed her to fulfill his psychological need. In other words, she soothed his frame of mind.

Second, the attraction that Jacob had for Rachel was much more than a physical attraction. He was attracted to her spirit; her inner beauty.

...even the ornament of a meek and quiet spirit, which is in the sight of God of great price.

I Peter 3:4

A mere physical attraction would never have endured the number of years Jacob served before being able to take Rachel as his bride.

Thirdly, Samson's love for Delilah was superficial, an obvious physical attraction. His words "saw" and "seen" attests to that.

Three needs were met: Isaac had a psychological need that was met by Rebekah, Jacob had a spiritual need that was met by Rachel, and Samson had a physical need that was met by Delilah.

God knows the needs of man. Adam was created a three-part being; spirit, soul and body. When God created Adam, he knew that Adam would need a helpmate to complement these three unique needs. In order to accomplish this, God created marriage. This is why the wife's role in the marriage is extremely important.

> **And the Lord God said, It is not good that the man should be alone; I will make him an help meet for him.**
>
> **Genesis 2:18**

As always, God honors His Word. He provides marriage as a means to honor His Word by giving man a helpmate.

Marriage is ordained by God. The concept of marriage is honored by God.

> **What therefore God hath joined together, let no man put asunder.**
>
> **Mark 10:9**

What has God joined together? The concept of marriage which is perfect because God is perfect. Everything he creates is perfect. God's thoughts of marriage are perfect. His thoughts of marriage is not like ours.

> **For my thoughts are not your thoughts, neither are your ways my ways, saith the Lord.**
>
> **Isaiah 55:8**

The Word of God gives instruction and order for marriage to conform to his thoughts of marriage. Another reason why God's concept of marriage is perfect because it joins together the three unique needs of man and woman: spirit, soul and body. By this union, man and woman become whole and together they become one flesh. Their spirits and souls are united and the union is consummated in the natural. It is more likely that this marriage will endure because of the orderly bonding and connecting that have occured. This order is the will of God.

> **Therefore shall a man leave his father and his mother, and shall cleave unto his wife: and they shall be one flesh.**
>
> **Genesis 2:24**

Communication, respect and trust are key for a healthy marriage, in addition to genuine love. Don't hesitate to discuss uncomfortable, sensitive issues, or, what may appear to be embarrassing subject matter.

Don't prejudge each other's response to issues you want to discuss. You may be surprised to discover that your mate is receptive to the discussion.

Make your mate aware of words or actions that have caused you hurt before they lead to scars and bitterness. Communicate these feelings to each other. Take them to the Lord in prayer.

> **He healeth the broken in heart, and bindeth up their wounds.**
>
> **Psalms 147:3**

Apologize when you are in error so that your communication will not be jeopardized.

Also, there are some practical things that should be addressed, such as, hygiene and physical appearance.

Even though I Peter 3:1-6 places emphasis on the qualities of the inner spirit, it does not suggests neglect of the physical appearance. There must be a healthy balance between the emphasis placed on the qualities of the inner spirit and the outward adorning. Common sense should be used when it comes to physical fitness.

If our bodies are not functioning well and are always sick and weak, we can not give our best to each other or to God; after all, our bodies first belong to God.

> **Know ye not that ye are the temple of God, and that the Spirit of God dwelleth in you?**
>
> **I Corinthians 3:16**

The inner qualities of the spirit are very important, however, a clean, healthy and fit body will add another dimension to the appeal and total attraction for each other. After all, we want to be looked upon as Kings and Queens in each others' eyes.

Maintaining your marriage should be your goal.

Treat it like you would treat gold. Pursue it with passion and drive. It is your vision and your dream. Keep it in the forefront, and never lose sight of it. Always keep it nourished and watered.

Think of your marriage as a young, tender house plant sitting in a pot. The plant becomes dry so you water it. The thirsty plant absorbs all of the water so you quickly replenish it with more water until you are sure its water supply is sufficient to quench its thirst and nurture it.

You go through this process repeatedly throughout the duration of the life of the plant. **You** determine the life span of the plant. If you stop watering the plant, it will die.

Will you nurture the plant so that it will live and grow, or will you allow it to die?

Your marriage needs to be watered continuously; over and over again in order to thrive, grow and live. At times, it will even need something extra, like fertilizer. Commit every area of your marriage to God.

> **Commit thy works unto the Lord, and thy thoughts shall be established.**
>
> **Proverbs 16:3**

A popular wedding gift selection is a set of "his" and "her" towels. Over the past several years, this trend has expanded to include new houses being built with "his" and "her" toilets, sinks, and closets. In maintaining this trend; "his" and "her" prayers are in order, followed by a prayer in unison.

Prayer for Marriage:

His: Heavenly Father, I commit my total being to you and acknowledge you in every area of my life, especially as a husband. My desire is to love my wife just as Christ loves the Church, His body, and gave His life for it. I want to possess the qualities necessary to be the husband you would have me to be so that I may live joyfully with my wife all the days of my life.

I want to cleave unto my wife, dwell with her and honor her according to your Word because we are one flesh.

I pray for a spirit of submission so that I may hear and receive advise, wise counsel, or insight as you will.

Let me always be looked upon as a King in (insert name) eyes. Give me the wisdom to be mindful of what I must do to keep my body healthy and my mind and thoughts sound so that (insert name) will always see me as her King, in Jesus' name. Amen.

Hers: Heavenly Father, I commit my total being to you and acknowledge you in every area of my life as a wife and a helpmate. My desire is to submit myself unto my husband as unto the Lord.

I pray that (insert name) will always think of me and treat me like a precious jewel and that I will always demonstrate the necessary qualities so that he will want to think of me and treat me like a precious jewel.

My desire is to display a meek and quiet spirit which is in your sight of great price, and to be virtuous, modest and gracious.

Let me always be looked upon as a Queen in (insert name) eyes. Give me wisdom to be mindful of what I must do to keep my body healthy and my mind and thoughts sound, in Jesus' name. Amen.

Both: Heavenly Father, the desire of our hearts is that this marriage bring glory and honor to your name. Therefore, we commit this marriage to you. We trust in you and know that this marriage will be successful.

We pray for insight to become more knowledgeable of each others' ways and habits. Give us wisdom to discern when to communicate and how to communicate so that our marriage will possess the necessary qualities to be honorable in your sight.

We pray for compassion towards each other and desire to be heirs together so that our prayers will not be hindered. We want our thoughts towards each other to be good thoughts.

We desire to cultivate and nurture our marriage so that it will become the kind of marriage that you, our Heavenly Father, ordained in Heaven. We thank you that our marriage is protected on every side, in Jesus' name we pray. Amen.

Think on these things:

I am a gem.
Genuine love begins within.
To love another,
I must first love myself.

CHAPTER 8

GOD OF PEACE

When thou liest down, thou shalt not be afraid: yea, thou shalt lie down, and thy sleep shall be sweet.

Proverbs 3:24

A tempest is a severe storm. Many references of such conditions are illustrated in the Bible. Whenever a strong wind occurred, a change took place in the lives of those effected. The impact of the wind affected all that it came in contact with.

I Kings 19:11 gives an account of a strong and mighty wind that was so powerful it destroyed a mountain. Another great wind caused a house to collapse which took the lives of Job's sons (Job 1:19).

Jonah's life was changed by the forceful wind which tormented the ship he boarded to run away from the presence of God. Not only was his life influenced by the wind, but the lives of all on the ship were in jeopardy. The total destruction and loss of the ship was at stake (Jonah 1:3-4).

Paul's warning to delay sailing because of contrary weather conditions and impending fierce winds, was not heeded. Many lives were at the mercy of this severe storm because of the devastating impact of the wind (Acts 27:9-11).

The wind represents those intense disturbances

which come into our lives unexpected and unplanned. They come with the commotion and force of a roaring cyclone, empowered to uproot us from our course if we are not grounded and founded in our God of Peace.

> **We are troubled on every side, yet not distressed; we are perplexed, but not in despair; Persecuted, but not forsaken; cast down, but not destroyed.**
>
> **II Corinthians 4:8-9**

Jesus was able to sleep in the midst of a great storm of winds and waves that beat into the ship where he lay. An account of this is given in Mark 4:35-39. He was able to sleep because he knew his God, a God of Peace. What was good enough for Jesus should be good enough for us.

> **And the God of peace shall bruise Satan under your feet shortly ...**
>
> **Romans 16:20**

Jesus displayed the perfect peace that he spoke of in John 14:27, "Peace I leave with you, my peace I give unto you: not as the world giveth, give I unto you." Romans 16:20 assures us that Satan is under our feet. Jesus Christ is the victor, therefore, we have the peace of God in our lives. Jesus Christ bore our griefs and sorrows.

> **These things I have spoken unto you, that in me ye might have peace. In the world ye shall have**

tribulation: but be of good cheer; I have overcome the world.

John 16:33

Imagine Jesus in the ship surrounded by a great and mighty storm of wind and fierce-powerful waves beating into the ship; yet he lay asleep on His pillow. He knew His God of Peace. He spoke three words, "**Peace be still**." At this command, the wind ceased and there was a great calm.

When you experience restless, sleepless nights, a soothing-tranquil effect will consume and overcome you as you meditate on the example that Jesus set. Keep your mind on him. Peace belongs to you.

Command peace into your life. Speak peace over every situation. Lull yourself to sleep as you lay on your pillow with the same confidence that Jesus displayed; assurance in the Almighty God of Peace. Hallelujah!

Thou wilt keep him in perfect peace, whose mind is stayed on thee: because he trusteth in thee

Isaiah 26:3

This prayer will have a tranquil influence on you. I can, personally, attest to it. During the course of me writing this book, I was faced with many obstacles to hinder its completion. Tempest storms were constantly pushing against my door. In the middle of sleepless, restless nights, I would awaken and pray this prayer. It soothed my thoughts and anxieties and gave me rest and assurance in Jesus Christ. I fluffed-up my pillow and slept.

Prayer for Peace: Thank you Heavenly Father for being my God of Peace. Your peace protects me so that I won't become distracted and overwhelmed by the things of this world. Your peace is my shield and refuge and keeps me from all thoughts of fear, worry and anxiety.

Your peace keeps my heart and mind through Christ Jesus, therefore, I will think on things that are true, honest, just, pure, lovely and of a good report.

Thank you for providing me with rest on every side, so that I won't be moved by adversity nor evil occurrences. The Lord is my Shepherd and leads me into green pastures and still waters.

I am free from distress and despair because Jesus said, "Be of good cheer, I have overcome the world." I am kept in perfect peace because my mind is on Jesus Christ, the victor and the giver of peace. I acknowledge you as my God of Peace, in Jesus' name. Amen.

Think on these things: Jehovah-Shalom (God of Peace). I am never alone

CHAPTER 9

GOD OF YOUTH

Lo, children are an heritage of the Lord: and the fruit of the womb is his reward. As arrows are in the hand of a mighty man; so are children of the youth.

Psalms 127: 3-4

Children are a gift of God. He graciously gives them according to Genesis 33:5. My favorite definition of gracious is: marked by kindness, merciful, compassionate and **generosity of spirit.**

And he took them up in his arms, put his hands upon them, and blessed them.

Mark 10:16

Because they are of such great value, God has a specific plan for their lives.

Before I formed thee in the belly I knew thee; and before camest forth out of the womb I sanctified thee, and I ordained thee a prophet unto the nations.

Jeremiah 1:5

He also gives specific instructions to parents to teach, train, provide for and nurture in love.

Train up a child in the way he should go: and when he is old, he will not depart from it.

Proverbs 22:6

How does a parent train a child? Parents should have the Word of God in their hearts so that they can be taught to their children (Deuteronomy 6:5-9).

And thou shalt teach them diligently unto thy children, and shalt talk of them when thou sittest in thine house, and when thou walkest by the way, and when thou liest down, and when thou riseth up.

Deuteronomy 6:7

Parents are encouraged to be **diligent** in their teaching. The word diligent is defined as: steady, earnest and energetic. Parents are to teach, train, provide for and nurture in love.

God wants mothers to be joyful of their children (Psalms 113:9) and he wants fathers to be happy and not ashamed (Psalms 127:5). Children are admonished to hear and obey the instructions of their parents. In order for the children to hear and obey the instructions, the parents must give the instructions.

Children obey your parents in the Lord: for this is right.

Ephesians 6:1

Children, obey your parents in all things: for this is well pleasing unto the Lord.

Colossians 3:20

The purpose of the training, teaching and

nurturing is to prepare children for young adulthood. There comes a time when children are no longer children and must be released.

I received these words of wisdom from God at a timely period in my own life in dealing with my own young adult.

RELEASE YOUR YOUNG ADULT

There is a level of innocence in a child's life. The parent stands between the child and God, sort of like an advocate or an intercessor. During this time, the child is innocent, naive and depends totally upon the parent. As the innocence and naivety diminishes and the child becomes less dependent upon the parent, the child will need to answer to a **higher authority**. **That higher authority is God.** The parent will no longer be the intermediary. The child is no longer that sweet, little innocent person you once knew. But has now acquired knowledge, and, hopefully, through parental training and influence, has also received spiritual awareness through Jesus Christ.

The parent is no longer making decisions for the child. Therefore, the parent will no longer be held accountable. The child is no longer a child but a young adult making decisions for his or her **own** life, and, therefore, must be held accountable for those decisions.

However, the accountability is no longer to the parent but is now to a higher authority, God! The young adult has now advanced and has been elevated to a new position to **"GO DIRECT"**, answer to and be in direct contact with the greatest higher authority there is.

So, release your young adult and accept his or her new position in God. Rest, relax and enjoy the freedom. You, as a parent, are now free.

It's time for a celebration; there's been an elevation.

Any conflict between you and your young adult will begin to diminish once you relinquish the control to God. Your relationship will become warmer and friendlier. You will no longer be the "enemy".

A battle occurs between the young adult and the parent when this release does not occur. The young adult wants to be loosed from the parent's control, but the parent wants to retain control. There's a tug-of-war which causes tremendous friction and tension. Neither young adult nor the parent can appreciate the other during this time.

It's time for a celebration; there's been an elevation.

Release your young adult and celebrate. God is in control.

The battle has been won, so start having fun.

Your part is done.

Young adults should not be deprived of the opportunity

to personally know their Heavenly Father. They can only develop this kind of relationship when they are released and allowed to make decisions and mistakes. They will learn to depend on God, not on themselves and not on their parents.

The young adult will now have an opportunity to grow and experience one of the most wonderful and exciting relationships that can exist: **A relationship with God.**

Prayer for Youth: Heavenly Father, we pray for a radical change in the heart's of all youth and in the direction of their paths. We pray for a radical change in the heart's of our cities, schools, universities and nation. Our cities will no longer be a Sodom or Gomorrah, but will be dedicated to the Lord Jesus. God Almighty, bond and raise up a remnant so that your will and purpose will be accomplished in the lives of all youth.

The young women will replace their revealing-scanty attire with robes of righteousness. Give them the desire to adorn themselves with the ornament of a meek and quiet spirit which is in the sight of God of great price. The young men will discard their weapons of knives and guns and will pick-up the weapon of God: the sword of the Spirit. The weapons of their warfare are not carnal, but mighty through God to the pulling down of strongholds.

We pray that they will humble themselves before you, pray, seek your face and turn from their wicked ways so that you will forgive their sins and heal the nation.

We bind spirits of lust, lasciviousness and immorality. The anointing will destroy and cast down desires for drugs, alcohol and any form of substance abuse. Their minds and bodies will be cleansed and purified by the blood of Jesus Christ so that they may be presented to you which is their reasonable service.

Your Word says that you will bring health and cure them. You will reveal an abundance of peace and truth to them and cause them to return to you and build them up as at first. Cleanse them from all their iniquity where they have sinned and transgressed against you. They shall be unto you a name of joy, a praise and an honor so that all nations will hear of the good that you have done towards them.

We pray that they will release all anger and bitterness so that their wounds and scars that have been caused by lies, harsh words and any form of child abuse will be healed by the healing balm of Jesus Christ. We rebuke violent spirits and replace them with the fruit of the Spirit: love, joy, peace, longsuffering, gentleness, goodness, faith, meekness and temperance.

All children shall be taught of the Lord, and great shall be their peace. In righteousness shall they be established. They shall be far from oppression and shall not fear. They shall be far from terror which shall not come near them.

Thank you for breaking the arms of their enemies and for scattering and dispersing every evil plot and kingdom set out to destroy them so that all will know that you are Lord. Be unto them a wall of fire.

They are a chosen generation, a royal priesthood, called out of darkness into the marvelous light to show forth the praises of God, in Jesus' name. Amen.

Think on these things: The youth are in the palm of God's hands.

CHAPTER 10

GOD OF PRAISE

Let the high praises of God be in their mouth, and a two-edged sword in their hand.

Psalm 149:6

Praise is the last chapter of this book. We use familiar expressions such as, "saving the best for last," and "the icing on the cake." Keeping those expressions in mind, **praise** is the best; **praise** is the icing on the cake. After every prayer, praise God for what he has already done.

Imagine your prayer as a cake which is now ready for the icing. You followed all of the directions to ensure that you used the right ingredients and that they have been properly mixed. You followed the exact recommended baking temperature and time. When you removed the cake from the oven, it was golden-brown, soft and moist. You touched it, and it sprung back into form. You baked a perfect cake which is now ready for the icing.

Be just as attentive and diligent in your prayer life. You can pray the perfect prayer; a prayer with results.

Ingredients:

Know the Word of God concerning your prayers so that you pray the **will** of God.

Teach me to do thy will; for thou art my God...

Psalm 143:10

Pray the Word of God. He hears and is faithful to perform His Word.

Let us hold fast the profession of our faith without wavering; for he is faithful that promised.

Hebrews 13:23

Believe what you pray. Have **FAITH!**

Therefore I say unto you, What things soever ye desire, when ye pray, believe that ye receive them, and ye shall have them.

Mark 11:24

Delight thy also in the Lord; and he shall give thee the desires of thine heart.

Psalms 37:4

PRAISE!

Praise is important because it executes vengeance upon the heathen, your enemies (Psalm 149:7).

There are many ways to praise God. Praise him with the sound of the trumpet, psaltry, harp, stringed instruments, organs, high sounding cymbals and dance (Psalm 150:6).

Let every thing that hath breath praise the Lord. Praise ye the Lord.

Psalm 150:6

Praise is an offer of sacrifice to God and the fruit of our lips giving thanks. God is pleased with our praises (Hebrews 13:15-16).

Where shall we praise him? Praise him in the congregation of the people and the assembly of the elders (Psalm 107:32). Praise him everywhere.

Who and **what** shall praise him? The Word of God reveals that hosts of angels, men, women, and children shall praise him. Furthermore, beasts, cattle, and all creeping things are included. The sun, moon, stars, heaven, waters and mountains shall praise the Lord (Psalm 148). Hallelujah!

Isn't it exciting to be included in one of these categories. Rejoice and praise the Lord. Praise him while you are able.

While I live will I praise the Lord: I will sing praises unto my God while I have any being.

Psalm 146:2

When shall we praise him? Praise him everyday, for ever and ever (Psalm 145:2). Praise him seven times a day (Psalm 119:164).

Why shall we praise him? To give thanks unto

the Lord.

O give thanks unto the Lord, for he is good: for his mercy endureth for ever.

Psalm 107:1

God redeems us from the hand of our enemy. He satisfies our longing soul with goodness. He calms the storm; he heals and delivers (Psalm 107).

Praise Him for His goodness, His wonderful works. He turns dry ground into water springs and sits the poor on high. His mercy is great above the heavens.

By him great wonders were performed: heaven and earth were established, mighty majestic waters were fixed into place. He provided the sun light to rule by day, the moon and the stars by night (Psalm 136).

Every man, woman and child have praise.

I Corinthians 4:5

Praising God has many benefits. You will miraculously be renewed and refreshed; mentally, physically and emotionally as you offer praise unto the Lord.

Before you pray the prayer of praise, you need to prepare your mind and your body to be free. Therefore, stand, stretch and release all of the tension from your mind and body.

Imagine yourself as a tree. You have been standing firm and rigid for a long, long time. You have been upholding and supporting many limbs, branches and leaves. You have been the tunnel through which they received nourishment from your roots. You have upheld them for years and years. You need to be renewed and refreshed.

Allow the Holy Spirit to move freely as you begin to praise. He wants to minister to you, to restore and renew you. He wants to be the tunnel to nourish you just as you have nourished. Release yourself and flow with God's Spirit.

Praise is worship unto the Lord. The Holy Spirit will lead you into such a praise, you will think you are in Heaven.

Prayer for Praise: Heavenly Father, my praise shall be of you. I will bless you at all times. Your praise shall continually be in my mouth. My praise shall always be of you.

Thank you for being the God of my praise. My mouth shall speak the praise of the Lord, and my flesh shall bless your holy name for ever and ever in Jesus' name. Amen.

Think on these things: I will be joyful in my praise to the Lord and cherish it like wisdom.

PRAISE IS MY POWER TO THE TOWER AND THE TOWER IS PRAYER!

* * * * * *

CONCLUSION

> **Therefore I say unto you, what things soever ye desire, when ye pray, believe that ye receive them, and ye shall have them.**
>
> **Mark 11:24**

Jesus Christ is sitting at the right hand of God making intercession on our behalf (Romans 8:34). As we pray, he pleads our case to the Father. He intercedes for us.

There will be times when we have to pray alone, without a prayer partner. Take advantage of Jesus' position. He is our prayer partner who is always available. He is our **mediator**.

> **For there is one God, and one mediator between God and men, the man Christ Jesus.**
>
> **I Timothy 2:5**

A mediator is one who takes on a middle position, as intermediary, to bring about accord by effecting and communicating. In the book of Joshua, Chapter 23, the nation of Israel was reminded that they had witnessed the "God of Battles" who delivered them and gave them possession of land. They were urged to be courageous, obedient and to cleave unto God.

There are certain things that God requires of you in order for your prayers to be effective. **Obedience** is the most important requirement. He also expects you to be diligent and faithful towards the thing you are praying for. In other words, do your part. For example, if you are praying for a financial breakthrough, begin to use common sense. Develop a budget, plan to get out of debt, begin saving and curtail unnecessary, extravagant spending.

If you are believing God for a health need, evaluate your life style. Consider your eating habits, weight, sleeping pattern, mental attitude and other pertinent factors contributing to your health status.

If you are believing God for marriage and family needs, talk to those experienced in these areas. Ask God to lead you to wise counsel. Read literature on the topics you are concerned about to get the information and knowledge you need to make prudent decisions. Don't be too proud to seek help and advice.

You may require the aid of others: counsel, physicians, financial planners. God has given us all gifts and talents to help one another.

Picture Jesus Christ as your prayer partner, touching and agreeing with you. The enemy has to flee.

> **...No man hath been able to stand before you unto this day. One man of you shall chase a thousand: for the Lord your God, he it is that fighteth for you, as he hath promised you.**
>
> **Joshua 23:9-10**

If one man can chase a thousand, imagine the magnitude of principalities and strongholds put to flight when Jesus Christ is our pray partner. The flight has to be faster than the speed of sound and light.

There are **weapons** formed against us.
These weapons are **principalities** and **strongholds**.

Hallelujah! This is the conclusion!

No WEAPON that is formed against thee shall prosper...

Isaiah 54:17

In the book of Ephesians, Chapter One, we are reminded that Jesus Christ has an exceeding greatness of mighty power towards us as he sits in the heavenly places.

Far above all PRINCIPALITY, and power, and might,and dominion, and every name that is named, not only in this world, but also in that which is to come: And hath put all things under his feet...

Ephesians 1:21-22

The Lord is good, a STRONG HOLD in the day of trouble; and he knoweth them that trust in him.

Nahum 1:7

Follow this order:

> Be obedient to the Word of God.
> **PRAY!**
> Do your Part.
> **STAND!**

After you have prayed and praised, Ephesians 6:13 says, *"... and having done all,* ***to stand****."*

Think on these things: Jesus Christ is above every principality and the Lord is a stronghold.

PRAYER FOR SALVATION

For God so loved the world, that he gave his only begotten Son, that whosoever believeth in him should not perish, but have everlasting life.

John 3:16

Heavenly Father, forgive me for my sins. I believe that Jesus died on the cross, was wounded for my transgressions and bruised for my iniquities.

I invite the Lord Jesus to come into my heart and to become the Lord over my life.

I accept the gift of your only begotten Son, Jesus Christ, so that I will have everlasting life. I confess with my mouth the Lord Jesus and believe in my heart that you raised him from the dead. I call upon the name of the Lord, therefore, I am saved.

ORDER PAGE

To order by mail:

Please send me __________ copies of The Power Tower at $8.00 per copy. (See the following for shipping and handling charges).

SHIPPING & HANDLING

$0 - $10	$2.00	Write for volume discounts!
11 - 50	$3.00	
51 - 100	$4.00	
101 - up	5%	

Price: $8.00 / book
Quantity ordered: __________
Total order:_________
Total Enclosed: ___________

NAME____

ADDRESS:____

CITY:______________________, STATE: ___________________

PHONE: eve. (   ) ______________ day: (   ) ______________

CHECK ENCLOSED____ MONEY ORDER ENCLOSED_____

PAYABLE TO: *JACQUELYN BRYANT*

MAIL TO: JACQUELYN BRYANT
P.O. BOX 423
ROSELLE, NEW JERSEY 07203